BILL AND RECEIPT ORGANIZER

Name: _______________

Phone: _______________

Bill and Receipt Organizer

Date	Expenses	Amount	Paid

Notes

Bill and Receipt Organizer

Date	Expenses	Amount	Paid

Notes

____

____

____

Bill and Receipt Organizer 

Date	Expenses	Amount	Paid

Notes

Bill and Receipt Organizer

Date	Expenses	Amount	Paid

Notes

____

____

____

Bill and Receipt Organizer

Date	Expenses	Amount	Paid

Notes

Bill and Receipt Organizer

Date	Expenses	Amount	Paid

Notes

Bill and Receipt Organizer

Date	Expenses	Amount	Paid

Notes

Bill and Receipt Organizer

Date	Expenses	Amount	Paid

Notes

Bill and Receipt Organizer

Date	Expenses	Amount	Paid

Notes

Bill and Receipt Organizer

Date	Expenses	Amount	Paid

Notes

Bill and Receipt Organizer 

Date	Expenses	Amount	Paid

Notes

Bill and Receipt Organizer

Date	Expenses	Amount	Paid

Notes

____

____

____

Bill and Receipt Organizer

Date	Expenses	Amount	Paid

Notes

Bill and Receipt Organizer

Date	Expenses	Amount	Paid

Notes

____

____

____

Bill and Receipt Organizer

Date	Expenses	Amount	Paid

Notes

Bill and Receipt Organizer

Date	Expenses	Amount	Paid

Notes

Bill and Receipt Organizer 

Date	Expenses	Amount	Paid

Notes

Bill and Receipt Organizer

Date	Expenses	Amount	Paid

Notes

Bill and Receipt Organizer

Date	Expenses	Amount	Paid

Notes

Bill and Receipt Organizer

Date	Expenses	Amount	Paid

Notes

Bill and Receipt Organizer

Date	Expenses	Amount	Paid

Notes

Bill and Receipt Organizer

Date	Expenses	Amount	Paid

Notes

Bill and Receipt Organizer

Date	Expenses	Amount	Paid

Notes

Bill and Receipt Organizer

Date	Expenses	Amount	Paid

Notes

Bill and Receipt Organizer

Date	Expenses	Amount	Paid

Notes

Bill and Receipt Organizer

Date	Expenses	Amount	Paid

Notes

Bill and Receipt Organizer

Date	Expenses	Amount	Paid

Notes

Bill and Receipt Organizer

Date	Expenses	Amount	Paid

Notes

____

____

____

Bill and Receipt Organizer

Date	Expenses	Amount	Paid

Notes

Bill and Receipt Organizer

Date	Expenses	Amount	Paid

Notes

Bill and Receipt Organizer

Date	Expenses	Amount	Paid

Notes

Bill and Receipt Organizer

Date	Expenses	Amount	Paid

Notes

Bill and Receipt Organizer

Date	Expenses	Amount	Paid

Notes

Bill and Receipt Organizer

Date	Expenses	Amount	Paid

Notes

Bill and Receipt Organizer

Date	Expenses	Amount	Paid

Notes

Bill and Receipt Organizer

Date	Expenses	Amount	Paid

Notes

Bill and Receipt Organizer

Date	Expenses	Amount	Paid

Notes

Bill and Receipt Organizer

Date	Expenses	Amount	Paid

Notes

Bill and Receipt Organizer

Date	Expenses	Amount	Paid

Notes

Bill and Receipt Organizer

Date	Expenses	Amount	Paid

Notes

Bill and Receipt Organizer

Date	Expenses	Amount	Paid

Notes

Bill and Receipt Organizer

Date	Expenses	Amount	Paid

Notes

Bill and Receipt Organizer

Date	Expenses	Amount	Paid

Notes

Bill and Receipt Organizer

Date	Expenses	Amount	Paid

Notes

Bill and Receipt Organizer

Date	Expenses	Amount	Paid

Notes

Bill and Receipt Organizer

Date	Expenses	Amount	Paid

Notes

Bill and Receipt Organizer

Date	Expenses	Amount	Paid

Notes

Bill and Receipt Organizer

Date	Expenses	Amount	Paid

Notes

Bill and Receipt Organizer

Date	Expenses	Amount	Paid

Notes

Bill and Receipt Organizer

Date	Expenses	Amount	Paid

Notes

Bill and Receipt Organizer

Date	Expenses	Amount	Paid

Notes

Bill and Receipt Organizer

Date	Expenses	Amount	Paid

Notes

____

____

____

Bill and Receipt Organizer

Date	Expenses	Amount	Paid

Notes

Bill and Receipt Organizer

Date	Expenses	Amount	Paid

Notes

Bill and Receipt Organizer

Date	Expenses	Amount	Paid

Notes

Bill and Receipt Organizer

Date	Expenses	Amount	Paid

Notes

Bill and Receipt Organizer

Date	Expenses	Amount	Paid

Notes

Bill and Receipt Organizer

Date	Expenses	Amount	Paid

Notes

Bill and Receipt Organizer

Date	Expenses	Amount	Paid

Notes

Bill and Receipt Organizer

Date	Expenses	Amount	Paid

Notes

Bill and Receipt Organizer

Date	Expenses	Amount	Paid

Notes

Bill and Receipt Organizer

Date	Expenses	Amount	Paid

Notes

Bill and Receipt Organizer

Date	Expenses	Amount	Paid

Notes

Bill and Receipt Organizer

Date	Expenses	Amount	Paid

Notes

Bill and Receipt Organizer

Date	Expenses	Amount	Paid

Notes

Bill and Receipt Organizer

Date	Expenses	Amount	Paid

Notes

Bill and Receipt Organizer

Date	Expenses	Amount	Paid

Notes

Bill and Receipt Organizer

Date	Expenses	Amount	Paid

Notes

Bill and Receipt Organizer

Date	Expenses	Amount	Paid

Notes

Bill and Receipt Organizer

Date	Expenses	Amount	Paid

Notes

Bill and Receipt Organizer

Date	Expenses	Amount	Paid

Notes

Bill and Receipt Organizer

Date	Expenses	Amount	Paid

Notes

Bill and Receipt Organizer

Date	Expenses	Amount	Paid

Notes

Bill and Receipt Organizer

Date	Expenses	Amount	Paid

Notes

Bill and Receipt Organizer

Date	Expenses	Amount	Paid

Notes

Bill and Receipt Organizer

Date	Expenses	Amount	Paid

Notes

Bill and Receipt Organizer

Date	Expenses	Amount	Paid

Notes

Bill and Receipt Organizer

Date	Expenses	Amount	Paid

Notes

Bill and Receipt Organizer

Date	Expenses	Amount	Paid

Notes

Bill and Receipt Organizer

Date	Expenses	Amount	Paid

Notes

____

____

____

Bill and Receipt Organizer

Date	Expenses	Amount	Paid

Notes

Bill and Receipt Organizer

Date	Expenses	Amount	Paid

Notes

Bill and Receipt Organizer

Date	Expenses	Amount	Paid

Notes

Bill and Receipt Organizer

Date	Expenses	Amount	Paid

Notes

Bill and Receipt Organizer

Date	Expenses	Amount	Paid

Notes

Bill and Receipt Organizer

Date	Expenses	Amount	Paid

Notes

Bill and Receipt Organizer

Date	Expenses	Amount	Paid

Notes

Bill and Receipt Organizer

Date	Expenses	Amount	Paid

Notes

Bill and Receipt Organizer

Date	Expenses	Amount	Paid

Notes

Bill and Receipt Organizer

Date	Expenses	Amount	Paid

Notes

Bill and Receipt Organizer

Date	Expenses	Amount	Paid

Notes

____

____

____

Bill and Receipt Organizer

Date	Expenses	Amount	Paid

Notes

Bill and Receipt Organizer

Date	Expenses	Amount	Paid

Notes

Bill and Receipt Organizer

Date	Expenses	Amount	Paid

Notes

Bill and Receipt Organizer

Date	Expenses	Amount	Paid

Notes

Bill and Receipt Organizer

Date	Expenses	Amount	Paid

Notes

Bill and Receipt Organizer

Date	Expenses	Amount	Paid

Notes

Bill and Receipt Organizer

Date	Expenses	Amount	Paid

Notes

Bill and Receipt Organizer

Date	Expenses	Amount	Paid

Notes

Bill and Receipt Organizer

Date	Expenses	Amount	Paid

Notes

____

____

____

Bill and Receipt Organizer

Date	Expenses	Amount	Paid

Notes
____
____
____

Bill and Receipt Organizer

Date	Expenses	Amount	Paid

Notes

Bill and Receipt Organizer

Date	Expenses	Amount	Paid

Notes

Bill and Receipt Organizer

Date	Expenses	Amount	Paid

Notes

Bill and Receipt Organizer

Date	Expenses	Amount	Paid

Notes

Bill and Receipt Organizer

Date	Expenses	Amount	Paid

Notes

Bill and Receipt Organizer

Date	Expenses	Amount	Paid

Notes

Bill and Receipt Organizer

Date	Expenses	Amount	Paid

Notes

Bill and Receipt Organizer

Date	Expenses	Amount	Paid

Notes

Bill and Receipt Organizer

Date	Expenses	Amount	Paid

Notes

Bill and Receipt Organizer

Date	Expenses	Amount	Paid

Notes

Bill and Receipt Organizer

Date	Expenses	Amount	Paid

Notes

Bill and Receipt Organizer

Date	Expenses	Amount	Paid

Notes

Bill and Receipt Organizer

Date	Expenses	Amount	Paid

Notes

Bill and Receipt Organizer

Date	Expenses	Amount	Paid

Notes

Bill and Receipt Organizer

Date	Expenses	Amount	Paid

Notes

Bill and Receipt Organizer

Date	Expenses	Amount	Paid

Notes

Bill and Receipt Organizer

Date	Expenses	Amount	Paid

Notes

Bill and Receipt Organizer

Date	Expenses	Amount	Paid

Notes

____

____

____